The No Fluff/No BS Blueprint

Turn Your
PASSION
Into A Thriving
BUSINESS

A Rookie Entrepreneur Start Up Guide

by Gundi Gabrielle

First Edition Paperback: December 2017

ISBN-13: 978-1981352388
ISBN-10: 1981352384

The Cataloging-In-Publication Data is on file with the Library of Congress.

*This is a **SassyZenGirl** Guide*

TABLE OF CONTENTS

Let's Get Started! - 7

The 3 Must-Have Ingredients - 17

STEP 1 - Your Game Plan - 31

STEP 2 - Niche Down Y'All - 41

STEP 3 - Bread & Butter Basics: Start a Blog - 49

STEP 4 - Publish a Bestseller - 56

STEP 5 - Learn to Crush it: Marketing Basics - 69

STEP 6 - Get the Bling Flowing - 85

STEP 7 - Explode your Brand - 97

Final Words - 109

BONUS Chapter #1:
How to Chill with the M-Word - 114

BONUS Chapter #2:
Sassyliscious Brand Explosion - 133

PLEASE NOTE:

Since resource links are not clickable in the print version, I created an online **Resources Page** *with direct links to all resources and articles mentioned in this book. Just open it now and keep it available while you read:*

SassyZenGirl.com/Blueprint-Resources

Let's get started!

Heya, stranger.....:)

Welcome & great to meet you here!

If you are reading this book, then you were probably fascinated by the idea of:

Turning your passion into a thriving business...

but might have wondered:

Sounds like a dream, but is it really possible?

Is there a system that anyone can learn or is this just for the lucky few?

The answer:

There is indeed a system and, yes, anyone can apply it and turn their passion into a business.

Is it easy and will it be quick?

Usually not.

Will you have to work hard and be willing to learn new skills - maybe even get out of your comfort zone?

Yep - very likely.

Is it a get-rich-quick scam?

Nope - absolutely not!

Everything taught in this guide is perfectly legit and includes the same principles used by most successful online entrepreneurs today.

So how then *can* you turn a passion - almost any passion - into a thriving business?

The short answer:

By GROWING A FOLLOWING of people who are passionate about the same thing as you and

providing them with regular expert content and help related to your passion!

Sounds like fun?

Well, it is and it can be very fulfilling.

__But how is that a business you might ask?__

Where does the **BLING** come in?

Here's the secret:

Once you have a passionate following of people who love your niche and topic as much as you do (or need it urgently), you can easily monetize that following through books, courses, coaching/ consulting, freelancing, affiliate products and even eCommerce...

...while - still having fun with your audience, providing awesome content, AND sharing your passion with them.

All - in - One!

Win-win for everybody.

Sound delish?

It sure is.

Now....

little ditty problem...

you might say.

HOW... - do you get that awesome following...?

If it was easy, everyone would do it.

I gotcha.

And that's where this snappy little guide comes in.

How DO you grow a passionate following that will eventually provide you with a regular income?

In a nutshell:

By using 1 or 2 of the unique, awesome platforms the internet has to offer, such as a:

- *Blog*
- *Amazon Kindle Publishing*
- *Podcast*
- *Youtube Channel*
- *eCommerce Store*
- *Social Media*

and then learning how to get noticed on each - aka "marketing" - AND keep your ardent followers engaged.

That's it.

Pretty much.

Well, if it's so easy why doesn't everybody do it?

Glad you asked.

Because most never bother with "M"...

and without "M":

Nada followers

And

Absolutely NADA BLING!

"M", of course, stands for "Marketing", a word that makes most people shudder and run the other way.

In fact, if that describes you, be sure to check out the **BONUS CHAPTER #1: "How to Chill With the M-Word"** at the end of this book.

You will love "M" afterwards and realize that you never really understood her or what she's really about.

* Hint: it's not about: being sleazy, pestering everyone you know or trying to convince people to buy something they don't want.

In fact, "M" is the VERY opposite of that and includes such awesome goodies as "creating win-wins", collaborating and helping people…

Wow - really?

Didn't expect that one, did ya…?

Now….before we go over the 7 steps…..two more quick things:

#1 - Who am I and why should you even listen to me?

Fair question: I'm a Top 100 Business Author and 9-time #1 Bestselling Author.

As an Entrepreneur, I run several 6-figure online ventures, including a publishing company, a travel blog (yep...that's my *"Zen Traveller Bali"* book ahead of *"Eat, Pray, Love"* & *"Lonely Planet"*):

Several affiliate/niche sites and **SassyZenGirl - #ClaimYourFreedom (SassyZenGirl.com)**, a platform that helps people from all walks of life turn their passion into a business and chill with "M".

All while traveling the world as a Digital Nomad and enjoying the freedom that running a passion business can bring.

Financial freedom, y'all!

Before all that, I was a classical conductor and concert organist/pianist and ran my own music company, a 200-member choir and orchestra. We performed at Carnegie Hall, for the Pope on St. Peter's Square and many other famous venues.

Since I LOVE freedom and independence more than anything and didn't want to deal with boards, investors or donations, I acted as both Music Director and CEO, PR Department, Booking Agent, Recruitment, etc.

I always enjoyed the marketing part and even though I didn't really know what I was doing back then, we usually played to full houses and enthusiastic audiences - without spending large amounts on PR. Rather through relationship building, creating win-win situations and leveraging other's audiences.

Very much the same techniques - as I would learn later - that form the core principles of successful online marketing today.

I actually filled Carnegie Hall without a marketing budget - with a 20 min. standing ovation to boot - all with those very same, simple principles.

Alrighty, enough about me.

#2 - Your 3 Must-Have Ingredients

Really important.

You need these 3 goodies in your bag:

3 Must-Have Ingredients

#1 - EXPERT TRAINING

That's right.

You are "going back to school".

Not a literal school and without exorbitant tuition fees, but if you want to succeed - and turn your passion business into a full time income within the next year - you better get your little booty trained, or this will be VERY tedious and SLOW.

> *"If you want to be successful, find someone who has achieved the results you want, copy what they do and you will achieve the same result."*
> **Tony Robbins**

Expert training is THE shortcut.

In that context:

Big BOOBOO: The Lottery Mentality

It's fascinating how many people enter cyberspace expecting quick riches and international fame.

All without training and just by "winging it" somehow.

You wouldn't dream of working as a doctor, architect, plumber or cook without proper training!

Then why would you think it is any different when building an online business?

The Good News...

Online training is:

- *Usually fun*
- *Much less expensive than college*
- *Much shorter time frame*
- *You start earning while you learn*

Do a good course or two, apply what you learn, and you can start earning a side income very quickly. Sometimes within weeks, certainly within months.

It is also very reasonable - if you apply yourself - to generate a solid full-time income within the next year.

Or less than that...

I don't know any other profession where you can say that!

Which brings me to ingredient #2:

#2 - The ENTREPRENEUR MINDSET

Another BIGGIE:

Whatever online venture you are planning - be it a blog, a publishing company, an eCommerce store, freelancing or consulting, etc. - you are now an entrepreneur!

Act like one.

Be a professional. Have a long term mindset. Clarify your Goals and then employ laserlike focus and discipline to achieving them.

It's not about who makes money the fastest. It's about who makes it the "longest". Meaning for the rest of your life.

THAT is freedom.

Treat this like your new career, because that's what it is.

Commit to becoming the best you can possibly be - a topnotch expert in whatever you do - and then don't stop until you get there!

#3 - FOCUS on PASSIVE INCOME

WHOA - take shelter....

Another biggie flying by....

Biggies everywhere now.

Whoops.

Ok -

FOCUS:

The internet has blessed us - yes, "blessed" us - with an unprecedented opportunity to create passive income streams with very little investment, risk, or even time input.

What is passive income?

Traditional examples are:

- *A pension*
- *Rental income from real estate*
- *Licensing fees*
- *Royalties (books, music, etc.)*
- *Interests and other investment income*

In other words, money that keeps coming in without you having to work for it - aka *NOT* "trading your precious time for money".

Cool?

You do the work ONCE in the beginning and then it's mostly set and forget with just a little maintenance here and there.

The internet has GREATLY increased the options for creating passive income streams and has made it much easier to build them. Here are the best known examples:

* Affiliate Marketing
Affiliate marketing means: you recommend a product on your website, course, book, etc. and get a commission when someone buys using your link. It is THE bread and butter method to generate passive income and every successful internet entrepreneur uses it, regardless of platform or business type.

You can use it in conjunction with your business - or - make it an entire business of its own. You might have heard of "Niche Sites"? - That's what I'm referring to.

Whatever you do, you NEED to become a Ninja at affiliate marketing!

You can make SO much more money if you do - and it's all passive income. Set and forget.

Don't worry - this can be learned.

Like with everything online, there is a step-by-step system - a method - for doing affiliate marketing. And below I will share a resource to get you started easily and painlessly.

* Self Publishing

In particular on Amazon where you can leverage the awesome marketing power of the biggest store in the world.

I found Kindle Publishing the *absolute fastest*, most effective way to start generating passive income streams and grow a following on auto pilot.

For entrepreneurship, I'm referring to a series of **NON** fiction how-to books in your niche.

I get daily new subscribers and social media followers on autopilot, sell affiliate products and have been able to generate a full time income within just a few months.

It is incredibly powerful - IF - you learn the marketing part well.

There is "**M**" again….

You REALLY need to chill with her.

The cool part:

Once again, there is a step-by-step system that anyone can learn and follow. That's why expert training makes *SUCH* a tremendous difference!

* Online Courses
Is like Publishing 10X!

IF - once again, you master "M" and learn how to crush it during a launch. This one's more of an advanced technique. Not something I would start with, but definitely one of THE big money makers down the road.

* Softwares
Another advanced technique.

Requires a significant up-front investment since you'll need to hire a programmer - and again - you better be an expert marketer by then to actually sell that bad boy.

So, not a beginner strategy, but a FUN thing to keep in mind for later. Also an App for your brand - wouldn't that be cool?

* eCommerce

Not completely passive since you'll be adding and changing products. But once you have a system down, you can have a VA (virtual assistant) do most of the daily maintenance and set up while you just have fun with finding great new products and growing your brand.

* Memberships & Subscriptions - also not entirely passive since you need to create new content to keep members happy, but that, too, can greatly be automated and outsourced, allowing you to only spend a few hours or days per month, while growing a massive monthly income stream through membership sites.

Why Passive Income?

Like - duh….

:)

Aside from the obvious, passive income streams can massively free up your time so you can focus on expanding and growing your brand.

Learn new things, add another platform (and again, become an expert) while not having to worry about paying the bills and having enough to live.

I feel ya there!

My newest book features **23 Passive Income Blueprint** that you can start right now, even as a total beginner without a large budget:

Need Money Right Now...?

Then you can start with a freelance option until your passive income streams are substantial enough to sustain you.

A great starter option is **Virtual Assistant** - aka "VA" in cyber cool.

Nope.

Not a secretary, though you can if you want.

You'll be assisting business owners and solopreneurs with whatever special skills you have that can be performed remotely - from the comfort of your home. Often at your own hours.

It's the latest rage and pay can be really good.

If you want a head start and land clients pronto, start by reading this article *(direct link on the resources page: SassyZenGirl.com/Blueprint-Resources)* to see what's involved.

Or - if you are ready to roll, but want some top notch training, this very inexpensive course will help ya crushin' it quickly *(see Resources page)*.

And this one's for **Pinterest VA** *(see Resources page)* - which is a great specialty to go into....

A great place to get freelance clients is Upwork and this article *(see Resources page)* on "Location Rebel" shows you how to crush it on that platform, even as a newbie.

Location Rebel Academy *(see Resources page)* is another great resource for Freelancer training, even if you are not a Digital Nomad.

And, of course, you can offer consulting services related to your niche if you aren't already.

So for immediate income, you can add a freelance option (ideally, related to your field). But ALWAYS keep your eye on Passive Income as the long term goal. Then you'll have the freedom to do whatever you want - when you want, how you want.

THAT's Freedom!

Now......that you've been so awesomely prepared...

Let's rock it with the 7 steps:

Step 1 - Your Game Plan

This will be FUN!

And nope...

We'll not write a stuffy business plan!

BUT...

Clarity and focus are important, so let's set some basic goals.

Ready?

Here it goes:

1) Your Target Income

What is your dream monthly income that would allow you to live comfortably without needing a day job and also cover extra expenses?

Pick a number.

It's not final and you can adjust it any time, but it's important to be specific and write it down.

2) Your Time Frame

Pick an *exact* date by which you intend to reach that monthly income. At a minimum go with 1 year, maximum 2 years.

Again, pick an exact date.

Hint: chances are you'll get there much faster, but you don't want to stress yourself too much and most of all, you want to give yourself the time to properly learn the basics and build a solid foundation. Once you have done that - and that beginning can sometimes be a little tedious - growth can happen very rapidly.

So, don't rush in the beginning, but have a clear date in mind to keep yourself focused.

3) Answer: WHY is this so important to you?
Oops…. - stop!

No thinking!

No rationalizing.

This has to be something that *deeply* touches you emotionally.

Gives you goosebumps just thinking about.

Maybe you want to travel the world or spend more time with your kids. Maybe you want to start or support a charity that you care deeply about. Maybe there is a hobby you never have enough time for or you want to adopt more rescue pets.

In other words, don't write what you "should", but what your *heart* tells you. Be *passionate*.

Your WHY will be your motivator and keep you moving when the going gets tough. Building a business comes with the occasional frustrations and certainly takes a lot of work and dedication.

If you don't have a powerful, *inspiring* reason for doing all this, chances are you won't make it - or stick with it - beyond the first excitement.

It is crucially important and will keep this fun!

Once you have defined the above 3 points, write them down in 1 sentence and keep it somewhere visible on a daily basis.

I usually put a sticky note on my laptop with any major goal I set and the results have been nothing but phenomenal. *(below is the simple note I used in the very beginning when a #1 Bestseller in the next 30 Days was a major goal - and it worked...;-):*

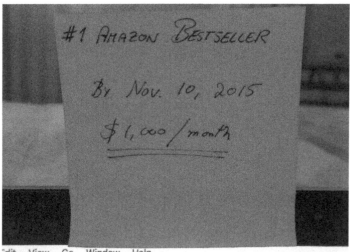

This little action brings one of the most powerful facilitators of success into the mix:

Laserlike Focus

Putting your goals & game plan in writing and having them in front of you on a daily basis, keeps you on track. Keeps you focused and will help you prioritize when you get overwhelmed.

That kind of focus also brings serendipity into play in a way that is often inexplicable.

Opportunities come your way out of nowhere. You come across just the right resource or article when you need it. You connect with people who can help you along.

Some people call it "Power of intention" or "Power of the Subconscious Mind", but labels don't really matter - the point is:

IT WORKS!

And I wouldn't start any major project without that kind of focus.

To be super duper clear…..

This little hack will NOT do the work for you. Not at all!

If you are lazy, stop reading.

Seriously.

But it **can** make things a lot easier and smoother - and keep you on track.

FOCUS IS EVERYTHING!

Especially when building a business.

Next, you'll break down your target amount based on the timeline you set:

How much do you need to make each day/week to achieve your target income?

Or - to use the above example, how many books, coaching sessions and affiliate sales, will it take to reach $1,000 per month?

Per day, per week, per month.

Have a number for each.

Once you divide your target amount into daily and weekly goals, it doesn't look so impossible anymore and you'll start getting ideas on how to achieve that number.

For a comfortable full time income, the numbers would, of course, be higher. I chose a part-time amount the first time around as that seemed easier to reach in a short time frame and then went on to higher numbers. Either way is fine, just pick one and go with it. Or use a combination of short and long-term goals - possibly even mid-term if you want to get super specific.

Don't get too carried away with this though. Keep it simple. Pick a number and then figure out how to reach that number with the following 6 steps.

Defining your Passion

The topic of this Blueprint is "turning your passion into a thriving business", so defining your passion is obviously another PRIMO factor.

If you already know what your passion is - great! You can move on to Step #2.

If you don't, try the questions in this article *(see Resources page)* to find some clarity. However, don't let the search stop you from starting your business.

It may take some time until you find your passion and it might really surprise you when you do. It certainly did for me - and it took me quite a long time to become clear on it:

Becoming a passionate entrepreneur and help others do the same. Teach internet marketing.....?

Seriously?

If someone had told me this years ago, I would have laughed (and it certainly isn't my *only* passion…).

It just never occurred to me, but I took action anyway, started with a travel blog, got into self-publishing and various other things - and eventually it just became obvious.In the meantime though, I had become an expert at marketing and knew the workings of the internet like a pro.

It was then very easy to explode my brand right out of the gate. Thank God, I didn't wait until I was clear on my main passion….

I also had no clue how much I would enjoy - truly enjoy - helping others in the creative process of building their business. And make it fun. An awesome adventure, rather than a tedious chore. Who knew?

So if you don't know what your passion is - GREAT! - it will be a fun exploration to figure it out and in the meantime:

START WITH SOMETHING!

Do NOT wait until you find your passion. Pick something and go with it.

Learn everything you possibly can on how to MARKET (see below), so that when you finally DO find your passion, you are ready to crush it and don't need to start from scratch.

Definitely pick something you enjoy - a hobby - whatever it may be, and use it as your practice tool.

Like with everything in life, practice makes perfect, and it will help you breach the learning curve.

Step 2 - Niche Down, Y'all!

Niche down time!

Cool jellies!

What the booty is she talking about?

Well...

Another Biggie flying your way.

Here it comes:

You NEED to find a super specific sub niche within your field that you become a specialist in.

Let that sink in…..

Because it's one of those things that will make or break you.

WHY?

Why bother?

Because the internet is super crowded already and it's almost impossible to get any traction if you are a jack-of-all-trades.

It is MUCH easier to find customers and grow a following in a super specialized subniche that you *dominate*.
Where you become the absolute go-to person that everyone refers to - and *links* to.

As an example, in the very crowded field of Life & Success Coaching, I knew of one guy who was absolutely crushing it as *the* "Quit Smoking" coach.

Can you see how that is MUCH easier to build a following for than a general motivation coach?

And how people will be more than happy to pay premium prices for that kind of specific coaching?

Another example was a guy who started a surf shop on Shopify. It didn't do well, because the competition was enormous - until...

...he started focusing on one special component on surf boards. Something that he became the absolute expert for. Where even world class surfers would come to him for advice and buy his products. Within a short time his languishing store exploded into 6 figures.

People LOVE to consult specialists and have them take care of their problems and needs.

And they are more than happy - *and expect* - to pay premium prices for that kind of specialized service.

So, find a specialized topic, niche or product in your field that is under-serviced. Something that people would love to have, but isn't really available - and then become the topnotch expert in that field.

How?

If you love your niche, you should already know most of the subniches.
You will also have a pretty good idea of what is under-serviced. There may even be something you always wished was available, that's really missing.

Be the one that fills that void.

Don't have the skills or knowledge?

Learn them.

It's usually not that hard and all the info and how-to's you could ever want can be found in:

The 2 Great FREE Universities called:
Google & Youtube

Yep - **"G" & "Y".**

Your 2 best friends.

From now on.

They'll help you become an expert in whatever field you want and they'll also help you with that iffy "R" word:

Re-search.

Yuk...

Let's make "R" more fun - shall we?

Here's how:

To get ideas, start subscribing to relevant, successful blogs in your niche and read the comments section. They can be a gold mine of information. Same with product or book reviews (especially the negative ones) and forums.

Find recurring themes that people keep complaining about or wish was available.

Forums, Facebook groups, Subreddits and even Quora questions can also be goldmines of information, plus you'll hear directly from your potential customers and readers!

Unfiltered!

The key here is:

1) find an under-serviced subniche *and then*

2) make sure it's something a large number of people *urgently wants* (or you will be wasting your time)

> *"Pay attention to what people care about, and reverse engineer it."*
> **Gary Vaynerchuk**

You can also create a poll for your friends on Facebook or in niche specific FB groups and forums.

Or you can ask open questions like:

> *"What is the #1 thing you are struggling with (niche specific)"*
> or
> *"What feature/service do you wish was available, but isn't yet?"*
> or
> *"What is your biggest frustration with......?"*

You will be amazed at the answers.

Things you never thought of.

In other words:

Don't ever assume you know what people want.

You don't.

Instead, always ask and *keep* asking.

Find out what people really urgently **need**, then provide it - and...

...enjoy a constant stream of dream followers, clients and customers on autopilot!

Without unpleasant pitching or selling involved.

In fact, they will come running to YOU, if you prepare this step well!

Keep playing with "R" for a bit. She means well. Give her a chance.

Keep fine tuning.

The more thoroughly you do this step, the easier everything else will be.

It is the FOUNDATION of EVERYTHING.

Step 3 - Bread & Butter Basics: Start a Blog

B & B = Bread & Butter Basic.

If you are new to the internet and the world of internet marketing, a **BLOG** is the easiest and least expensive way to get started and get your feet wet.

Plus, you will need one anyway - and a website. It's the bread and butter part of any business.

This free book *(see Resources page)* will help you set up your first blog painlessly and efficiently (no experience necessary).

This is actually the little book that started it all for me. My first #1 Bestseller (in those days, I still charged for it) and my first experience in freedom. Since then it has helped thousands of people start their first blog and it can do the same for you. Have fun with it. It is my free gift to you!

BooBoo Alerts:

#1 - do not go with a cheapy commercially hosted blog a la "Blogger, Blogspot, Wix, Weebly, Wordpress.COM" (not to be confused with the free software successful bloggers and entrepreneurs use: Wordpress.ORG)

Remember? You are an entrepreneur now. A professional!

Act like one and use - from the very start - the software that successful people use, not the cheapy hobbyist versions.

The book explains in-depth why, but it's such a classic Rookie mistake that it cannot be mentioned often enough.

#2 - Don't spend endless time over your domain name or the perfect design. I guarantee your design will change as you become more familiar with Wordpress - and most of all, as you understand more about how to design a website based on marketing principles.

So, try to pick a name that contains at least one relevant term (aka "keyword") related to your niche and get a decent starter design going.

※※※※※※

This should only take 10% of your time.

The other 90%, devote to:

#1 - Becoming an expert at **Blog Style Writing**

Here are two helpful guides *(see Resources page)*:

Henneke's 16 Snackable Writing Tips
(one of the best writers on the internet and some great, easy-to-digest tips)

Headline Hacks
(and everything else on that site....)

#2 - continue with **"R"** and become *really* knowledgeable about your niche.

Subscribe to at least 10 big, relevant blogs from your niche to get a sense of how *they* "do it" and to observe different ways of running a blog *successfully*. Also, observe their writing style, what appeals to you and why.

Not just their blog posts, btw, but also, very importantly, how they write emails….

#3 - Start building **Relationships with Peers & Influencers**

SO important - and right from the start. Be sure to check out **Rookie Mistake #8 HERE**:

SassyZenGirl.com/Cheat-Sheet-Rookie-Mistakes

......so you don't get yourself banned and ignored everywhere, but build awesome, productive - long term - relationships with your peers and major influencers in your field.

Take at least a month for this.

Write away, have fun with it.

And DON'T worry about followers and subscribers just yet.

You are in **Kindergarten**.

Enjoy this new adventure.

"Innocence is bliss" and there is no need to stress and put a lot of pressure on.

People will come when you are ready. Just chill for now.

Never lose sight of "P" though.

Your **Passion**!

And the reason **WHY** you are doing all this.

The beginning can be tedious and difficult at times, especially if you were not born with a tech gene (and couldn't care less... :)

Focus on your passion, your end goal.

Know that good things take time and they tend to grow slowly and steadily.

Not like weeds that shoot out quickly and then squash everything in their way.

Don't be a weed, yo..:)

Be a beautiful flower *(I know super fluff)*

and give yourself time to grow.....

and breathe.....

Difficulties, failures and frustrations will come and go.

That's for sure.

Everybody passes through them. That's part of life and certainly part of business.

You just take it one step at a time, build a solid foundation - and enjoy the journey!

Tom Ed, one of the coolest people ever, left us with this priceless quote:

"I'm not discouraged, because every wrong attempt discarded is another step forward."
Thomas Edison

Nothing more to say....

Step 4 - Publish a Bestseller

Before you say "BUT"....

Hear me out…;-)

And, btw, strike the "B" Word from your vocabulary.

For like EVER!

It's a total time waster and energy buster.

No use at all.

Especially in this context.

Cool?

Got it?

Good!

Now….

Publish a Bestseller...

YES - YOU can do this!

Even if you are not a writer and have limited time - and NO - it does not take years. You can do it in the next 30 days. Absolute maximum is 90 days (set your calendar - really!)

Why is this so important?

Because Kindle Publishing offers several tremendous benefits - *more* than any other marketing method I have seen.

It's like **business marketing on steroids.**

Here is why:

1) **the prestige of a published author**, and in particular a bestselling author, is priceless! Potential customers and clients will forever look at you in a different way and instantly trust you more as an expert - *and* be willing to pay Premium Prices.

2) Kindle Publishing allows you to **brand yourself as an expert & influencer** in a non-intrusive way.

Readers who love your style and find your information helpful will be *eager* to hire you or buy your services - and - will expect premium prices.

No "selling" needed.

How cool is that…?

3) In addition, Kindle Publishing is an **amazing list builder**.

We'll talk more about the importance of mailing lists in the money chapter, but for now I'll just say:

In my experience, Kindle Publishing has been *__the absolute fastest way to grow a list and following__* - completely on autopilot! - And you even get paid to build your list (aka "royalties").

Every morning when I look at my stats I'm shocked at how many more subscribers I have - completely on autopilot.

How is that possible?

Well, you can include a lead magnet (= freebie offer like a free checklist, free ebook, etc.) in the book and if it's a good one, interested folks will be happy to give their email address in return.

See how that works?

(See the Resourses page for a simple video tutorial on how to set up a *Sign Up Form to Mailing List* sequence).

4) You can **include affiliate offers** in the books (except Amazon products - those are strictly forbidden).

When you mention resources (softwares, tools, books, courses, etc.) in the context of explaining something, readers will often follow your recommendations and buy those products.

It's win-win for everybody: Your readers don't have to spend hours doing the research themselves, plus, they usually don't have enough knowledge yet to know what's best, and you are creating a passive income stream - on autopilot.

5) Successful Kindle books can become a great **funnel for future courses,** which is the 10X version of publishing in terms of income.

6) in the same line, Kindle books can be an amazing **funnel for your**:

* **Blog**
* **Podcast**
* **Youtube Channel**
* **Social Media**
* **Speaking Engagements**

Again, completely on autopilot. It's the fastest and easiest way to drive traffic to any of these ventures!

7) You are beginning to earn **passive income streams** from book royalties, especially if you also add print and audio.

There is a **BIG caveat** though:

All of the above applies **ONLY IF** the publishing and launching part is done right. And that's a big IF!

Many people have a bestseller these days, but very few books sell long term, which is, of course, the all important ingredient here.

It doesn't help your business much, if you have a great launch - and even a #1 Bestseller - if your book sinks into oblivion soon after.

Which is what happens to most books.

Pretty much 99% of indie published books - which is a pretty sad number.

The Good News:

There is a **step-by-step method** and it's not rocket science, but most indie authors either don't bother to learn or waste time on the many 2nd rate books and courses from people whose books don't sell either.

Don't be blinded if someone tells you they are a "Bestselling Author" - even #1 - because that's remarkably easy to do.

In most cases, if you check the Bestseller Rank = "ABSR" of their books, they will most likely be over 100K or much higher - meaning, they rarely ever sell a book (though they might have had a bestseller in the beginning as most people do these days).

The ABSR is the "Amazon Bestseller Rank" and can be found by scrolling down on the book's page - see here:

Product details

File Size: 1365 KB
Print Length: 228 pages
Page Numbers Source ISBN: 1544628773
Publication Date: March 9, 2017
Sold by: Amazon Digital Services LLC
Language: English
ASIN: B06XJ9MZVQ
Text-to-Speech: Enabled
X-Ray: Not Enabled
Word Wise: Enabled
Lending: Not Enabled
Screen Reader: Supported
Enhanced Typesetting: Enabled
Amazon Best Sellers Rank: #4,548 Paid in Kindle Store (See Top 100 Paid in Kindle Store)
  #1 in Kindle Store > Kindle eBooks > Arts & Photography > Photography > Reference
  #1 in Books > Business & Money > Marketing & Sales > Marketing > Industrial
  #1 in Kindle Store > Kindle eBooks > Arts & Photography > Music > Business

That number directly correlates with sales volume and unless the majority of an author's books are around 20K or lower (at the very least 30K) - they can't really teach you much. I'm not saying *every* one of their books needs to be in that range - and some genres sell better than others - but the majority of their books should be in that range and I mean books that have been out for a while (at least 3 months).

Same goes for the abundance of advice you hear in Facebook groups - again, check the author's ABSR and see if they walk the talk.

Another indicator of expertise is if an author is among the Top 100 of the ***overall*** category, like business, health, self-help, etc.

More about the author

› Visit Amazon's Gundi Gabrielle Page

Biography

**Top 100
Business Author
on Amazon**

+ Follow

Show More

Amazon Author Rank ^beta (What's this?)
#82 in Kindle eBooks > Business & Money

That is not easy to do and very few self-published authors can be found in those lists. If they do - absolutely listen to their advice and learn everything you possibly can from them. But it won't be that many, so be cautious who you listen to in this overcrowded market.

Once you get there, it's fun to see yourself outrank a lot of famous names (Brian Tracy, Russell Brunson and Robert Cialdini in the below screenshot) - without much ad spend. All through a smart launch and well thought out book set up.

THAT's when you've arrived and that's when Kindle Publishing can turn into the most phenomenal marketing machine on the internet!

The Method

Kindle Publishing - done successfully - has its own method and you *need* to learn that method *in-depth* to sell books long term.

It is absolutely doable and learnable for anybody - and it doesn't take a long time!

I had my first #1 Bestseller within 4 weeks, a book that kept selling well long after it was published and brought me many new subscribers, social media followers, client requests and affiliate sales.

It is not rocket science, but you NEED to learn it - or you will be wasting a lot of time and be disappointed quickly.

This Exclusive FREE Training Webinar will get you started:

Reserve your Spot HERE:
DreamClientsOnAutopilot.com

I'll show you the basic steps in a simple 4-Week Plan from zero to published - and also, how you can pretty much guarantee a #1 Bestseller even with your first book!

The other amazing thing about Kindle Publishing is that it is very inexpensive. Publishing on Amazon itself is free. You can even add a print version, completely free of charge with "POD" = "Print-on-Demand".

POD means you upload your text and cover files in pdf format and Amazon will only print a book when someone buys it.

Meaning, no up-front printing costs or boxes of books to store. A small printing cost is deducted from your royalties and Amazon handles everything, incl. Shipping!

Amazing, right?

Reach #1 for less than 500 Bucks!!

You can publish a book and have it reach #1 during launch week for less than $500 (costs would be for cover design, proof reading and launch week promos).

ALL the 7 benefits I mentioned above can start ***right away*** and keep coming in - IF you set it up right - while Amazon pays you royalties to build your business!

That's right!

Totally amazing. I don't know of any other marketing strategy that simple, inexpensive and effective!

So join me for the Exclusive FREE Training and jump start your business like a PRO!:
DreamClientsOnAutopilot.com

Step 5 - Learn to Crush it: Marketing Basics

We talked about this before.

AT LENGTH.

So I won't cover again why "M" is SO important.

Let's instead cut to the booty:

What - of all the many forms of internet marketing - should YOU be focusing on right now? - In addition, to Kindle Publishing, of course, which will usually be the fastest by far?

#1 - SEO
#2 - Guest Posting
#3 - Facebook Ads
#4 - Influencer Marketing
#5 - Collaborations with your Peers

That's it.

For now.

Let's have a closer look:

#1 - SEO
SEO (=Search Engine Optimization) is the science of how to rank in Google.

It's absolutely CRUCIAL that you learn this - and learn it well.

Especially, for affiliate marketing.

It is *mandatory* that you understand how SEO works and what you need to do - including structuring your site and articles.

This is non-negotiable.

SEO also applies to Youtube (another *formidable* marketing tool), Pinterest, Amazon, Etsy and various

other platforms. While each functions a little different, the main principles are always the same - and you need to master them.

While this *can* be a tedious subject at first, **my little Beginner SEO book (99c on Amazon)** makes this as painless as possible and brings you up to speed in a short 1-hour read.

You'll feel a lot better after that....

That's for starters.

Once you've got the basics, I recommend subscribing (free) to **Backlinko.com** - the foremost SEO blog on the internet - with amazing tips and resources.

Definitely start with some of these articles *(see Resources page)*, and keep reading at least one per week.

Onpage SEO: Anatomy of a Perfectly Optimized Page

Link Building the Ultimate Guide

The Definite Guide to Keyword Research

They are massive - each an absolute treasure - and fortunately, well written and fun to read. (You can also observe Brian's writing style as a **superb** example of how to blog REALLY well).

Don't stress on learning everything at once, but get the basics and then keep learning.

Consistently over the next year.

You are in this for the long run, right...?

SEO is one area where that really applies!

Success usually takes time, often a few months - but it's *well* worth it in the end, and it's important to start right away and not wait a year until you have time (you never will, by the way...:)

Local SEO
If you run a local blog or business, ranking #1 for your town/area - in particular, the top spot in the Maps - will be a great traffic source for you.

This step-by-step course by 7-figure SEO Chris Walker *(see Resources page)* - aka "Superstar SEO" *(really.... :)* - will show you in easy-to-follow steps how to do it. Chris has ranked hundreds of clients in the #1 spot - and kept them there for years to come. THAT's someone to listen to if you want your business to crush it locally!

#2 - Guest Posting

Big, Big, Biggie, Folks!

You NEED this one!

Getting an article published on a major blog or magazine can be a tremendous boost for your business, so including this in your beginner marketing arsenal is a must.

Obviously, you need to be a good writer and know how to pitch - and - what to write about.

But....

Once again, it's not as daunting as it seems.

There is, as always a system you can follow and in this case, I *do* recommend a course.

Actually THE course.

The one I found to be THE most important and valuable training I did during my early online career. My first year.

Fortunately, I took it right at the start and it was an amazing shortcut for everything else.

Not only for guest posting, but just as importantly, the writing training I received that was absolutely invaluable.

It also shaped how I write my books - in a more conversational blogging style - and was largely responsible for my quick success as an author.

AND - I learned how to chill with "R".

How to research viral topics. How to know what big blogs might be interested in and how to pitch them.

Without that course it would have been SO much more difficult and tedious.

It would have taken me MANY more months - vs. the 4 weeks for my first major guest posts on **Goodlife Zen** & **The Planet D**.

That's right.

4 weeks.... (and that included going through the training).

So unless you like wasting time or want to spend months on this, this is a no brainer and you can get yourself started here with a 30% discount:

Guest Blogging Course *(30% Discount)*
(see Resources page)

oh - I forgot to mention....

The creator, Jon Morrow, is not only one of the top bloggers in the world with a 7 figure blog of his own and an average of $7,000 per article when he still wrote guest posts, but....

...he is also paralyzed from the neck down....an amazing, inspirational story....)

Guest posting is also hugely important for book and product launches, or to promote your services.

And....

If you ever want to get those super cool press credentials a la: "As Featured On" or "As Seen On"....

This is how you get them: through guest blogging.

Or....

By spending thousands of dollars on a publicist.

Your choice.

To get you fired up....

Here are the requirements for guest posts on some of the most famous publications in the world:

Submission Requirements for Top Blogs like Forbes, Entrepreneur & Business Insider
(see Resources page)

Feel free to pitch them on your own....:)

Or just get the training - and get crackin'...

Your choice.

#3 - Facebook Ads

This might surprise you, but Facebook Ads are another must, also for your long term business.

You will definitely use them at some point and the most effective techniques are rather complex and take time to learn and really master.

So, start with something simple: "Boosting" your blog posts from your Facebook Fan page.

This little video shows you how
(see Resources page)

What about Social Media???

…you might ask.

And rightfully so. Everyone's talking about them and telling you how important they are.

Well - they can be….

But you can't do everything.

Certainly not learn everything all at once.

Remember FOCUS?

One of those really cool "F"-Words?

That's what it's all about and while social media can be an awesome way to grow your business, focusing on boosting a few posts on Facebook to start generating a following, is really all you need to do right now.

Unless....

There is one platform you absolutely LOVE and always hang out anyway.

In that case, sure.

Include that one.
It won't feel like a tedious chore and you are probably doing it anyway, so go for it.

There are also a few fields, where a particular social media platform is absolutely crucial - like Instagram for travel and Pinterest for Etsy - or in some cases Youtube.

In that case, of course, really focus on that platform and learn from the top influencers on how to market there. Those who make 6-7 figures off that platform and have and large and active following. Once again, expert training is the shortcut, so don't just create a profile with a few posts and hope for the best.

It-will-not-work!

The two to focus on would be Instagram and Pinterest and on the Resources page you can find some top training for each:

FREE Instagram Training(*)

100K/month with Pinterest(*)

Otherwise though:

Kindle Publishing - when done right - will be a much faster (and inexpensive) way to grow an audience AND get new social media followers on autopilot.

Right from the start!

I don't know about you, but I prefer the direct, most effective way, so that would be my recommendation.

Social media are a continuous effort and can be a massive time sucker, especially in the beginning of your online career.

Time that could be better spent learning new skills, working with clients and creating more income-producing assets (aka passive income).

In other words, time to grow your business effectively, rather than getting lost on Social Media.

#4 - Influencer Marketing

#4 and #5 cover the all important art of relationship building.

With influencers, you need to be patient.

Start getting on their radar by subscribing to their blog and regularly comment under their posts, social media, videos, etc.

Key here is to have something interesting to say and really make an effort.

Over time, these influencers will take notice of you and will then be much more open to support you, too, and share your content in a tweet (as an example). Or even link to one of your posts from their articles (aka "backlink").

Treat this like you would any relationship that is really precious to you. Don't squash it by asking too much too soon. And don't expect help or support when you haven't given any first.

Influencers are busy and get bombarded with emails every day. Most of them time wasters, pushy and needy, and quite tiresome after a while. Be among the few that stand out for their professionalism and respectful behavior. And, of course, your expertise.

Steady does it.

If you do, the rewards can be absolutely amazing.

#5 - Collaborations with Your Peers

Also relationship building, but this one will be easier. With peers, you want to look for win-win situations. Sharing each other's content with your audiences.

Guest posting or podcasting exchanges. Collaborations.

Also giveaway campaigns for authors or Summits/ Facebook Events that you organize together or appear on each other's events.

Unless someone has *exactly* the same product & audience as you (which is very rare), don't see your peers as competition, but rather as wonderful opportunities to collaborate, grow your businesses together and make each other more money.

The bigger and enthusiastic your network, the faster you will grow.

There are few things more powerful (and inexpensive) than leveraging other people's audiences!

You might know the term "OPM" from Real Estate: "Other People's Money".

It's a similar concept here: "OPA" - "Other People's Audiences". Except, you participate in the giving and sharing.

It's a 2-way street.

Start building those foundations early on - and never stop. You can never have too many connections.

Always start by finding ways to help and provide value to the person you are approaching. That attracts reciprocity and you will see your business grow in amazing ways.

Simple Productivity Hack

In that context, here is a simple strategy to not get overwhelmed:

Laserlike Focus!

Focus on 1 or 2 things at a time (maximum 3) and *really* give them your all and MASTER them.

Keep it simple.

Steady does it.

Step by step.

Only once you've mastered 1 or 2 and can automate most of them, is it time to move on to the next.

Otherwise, you'll get overwhelmed, frustrated and start wasting time on productivity books. Instead of using that time to build your business:

#1 - Start a Blog

#2 - Publish your first few Books *(Kindle books are short. You can easily publish 1 per month or every 2-3 months to keep growing a portfolio)*

#3 - Add SEO and Guest Blogging

#4 - Build Relationships with Influencers & Peers

Do that for the first 3-6 months - and see the magic happen.

If you can - without getting overwhelmed - by all means, include 1-2 social media accounts without going crazy.

But really focus on the above 4 points and ***master*** them.

Step 6 - Get the Bling Flowing

BLING-BLING!

FINALLY - we get to the good stuff:

MUCHO BLING - and how to get it!

As a beginner, the #1 strategy - aside from Kindle Publishing - will be:

#1 - Affiliate Marketing

I briefly mentioned AM in the intro:

You recommend products on your blog and receive a commission whenever someone buys.

A great source of passive income when set up right.

First, you'll want to find products in your niche that you would be *excited* to promote.

Ideally, products you use yourself.

A great place to start is *Amazon*. Just go to their site and put in keywords related to your niche and see what comes up.

Are there any products you are genuinely excited about that you could see yourself recommending?

Are their prices high enough to earn you a decent commission?

What do the reviews say? (very important)

Once you find a few, I would recommend buying the product and testing it out for yourself.

Then write a review post, describing all the pros and cons and include your affiliate link.

First, of course, you need to sign up with *Amazon*'s **Affiliate Program** and then get a "hop-link" for each product (Affiliate-Program.Amazon.com)
That's a url with your particular affiliate ID.

Whenever someone clicks on it, a cookie will be installed on that person's browser and **anything** that person buys on Amazon within the next 24 hours will earn you a commission! - **not just** the product you are recommending!

This is great, though keep in mind that *Amazon*'s commission rate is overall very low and their rules are extremely strict. Violate them even once and your account might get banned forever.

This article will give you the gist of it *(see Resources page)*.

And here are several free beginner guides from some of the top online Ninjas around *(see Resources page)*:

NicheHacks
Amazon Affiliate Ultimate Guide

ShoutMeLoud
Amazon Affiliate Beginner Guide

Other well known affiliate programs are *Clickbank, Commission Junction, JVZoo and Udemy* (for courses). Also, countless company owned programs like softwares or web hosting companies - and - the big, and very lucrative, arena of online courses.

That's where the big money is with commission rates of usually 50%. (Yes, of the sales price.....)

Some will give you 30% which is still a nice chunk.

I wouldn't go for less than that and like I said "industry standard" for courses - and most softwares - is 50%.

To be super duper clear:

If you recommend a $500 course and someone buys it using your link, you could be making $250 - just like that!

WHOA!!!

Yep, exactly!

The idea here is to automate the process by having the link in a review post or a banner in the side bar (or within a post) - and then - driving enough targeted traffic (aka interested people in your niche) to your site.

You don't actively "sell" or talk to them, you just keep the traffic flowing in and have that course visible enough for people to find.

Once you perfect that, it becomes money on auto-pilot.

"While you sleep"....as they say....

Got it?

A "Resources" or "Recommended Tools" page on your blog is another great place for affiliate products.

Readers love them. Just be sure to disclose your affiliate status. You are required by law - well, the FTC....

To find all the awesome affiliate offers in your niche, ask Big "G" for help.

Here is how:

Google your niche and the word "affiliate program" or a specific product you like with "affiliate Program" and see what you can promote.

Also, check *review posts* and *resources/tools pages* on the top blogs in your niche.

They usually list them ALL!

That's a quickie way to find the good ones - and avoid the time wasters.

In the beginning…

I would pick 2 or 3, start with review posts and put a banner in the side bar or somewhere within your blog text.

Be sure to pick quality products you can *full heartedly* recommend.
People will trust your judgement and recommendation, so make sure you honor that trust.

Here are some great free beginner guides on Affiliate Marketing *(see Resources page)*:

Neil Patel
Ultimate Guide to Affiliate Marketing

ProBlogger
3 Ways to increase Affiliate Income for Bloggers

And an awesome course on the Resources Page:

50K per Month with Affiliate Marketing!(*)

Once again, one of the easiest and fastest ways to drive traffic to your affiliate products will be **Kindle Publishing**. I know I'm repeating myself (sorry..:) - but it is really THAT amazing and fast.

What about Selling Ad Space?

That's more of a Boo-Boo these days (though there are exceptions).

Here is why:

Sites with lots of ads tend to look spammy, and not just to visitors, but also to Google.

Meaning….

It can potentially harm your ranking, because Google's algorithm has shifted focus much more towards quality. You want to avoid anything that looks spammy - unless you are a major, high authority site.

(You are not, in case you are wondering....:) - not yet, anyway.

Also, payout is usually not very high - especially as a beginner, so these days cool bloggers focus mostly on affiliate marketing and product sales.

If you want to check it out though, one of the better companies is **Mediavine.com**.

And here is some more food for thought on the subject as shared by some of the top blogs *(see Resources Page)*:

SmartBlogger:
13 Reasons Why Blog Ads Suck For Monetizing Your Site

BlogTyrant:
Don't Put Ads On Your Blog

ShoutMeLoud:
Can Bloggers Make Money Without Google Adsense

#2 - Sell your Products

Obviously....

...if you already have products, especially digital products, you can sell them through your blog and books. If you don't, not to worry - you will soon....

If your niche lends itself to consulting or coaching, then by all means, offer that service.

While you should long term focus on passive income, freelance gigs are a great and quick way to generate money while you focus on improving your marketing chops and growing your brand.

And you might just LOVE coaching and consulting - like I do....

So even with solid "passive" income streams, you might continue freelancing just because you enjoy it so much.

Now - isn't THAT a fun idea?

Your most important Asset

Get ready:

Drum Roll!!

Here it comes:

One of your most important business assets will always be:

Your **MAILING LIST!**

And don't take it from me.

EVERY successful internet entrepreneur, blogger, or author will tell you the exact same thing.

Why?

Because that is the one PR asset you OWN.

Amazon might change their rules, so might Google, so might Facebook or any other social media platform.

Any other venue you use to connect with your following.

The only one you have complete control over (aside from your website), the one you truly OWN, is your mailing list.

So growing that, NURTURING that - will be one of THE most important parts of your "E" - Journey (E for Entrepreneur).

Once you do and your readers like and trust you, you can occasionally (emphasis on *occasionally!*) recommend a course or product to them (aka Affiliate Marketing) and they will be much more likely to buy than from a complete stranger.

Same when you offer a new service or have a book launch coming up. An active mailing list can be amazing and jump start any new project!

You can also conduct surveys and get feedback from your readers on a regular basis. That feedback will help you tailor your content, product and services, so you can always be sure that whatever you create will have an enthusiastic audience.

Rather than guessing and hoping for the best, which is what most people do.

Your list is also invaluable for JV webinars (joint venture) where you allow someone else to present their product or service to *your* list while you get a commission for every sale made as a result of that webinar (another form of Affiliate Marketing!)

Step 7 - Explode your Brand

The secret to exploding your brand after you've built a solid foundation is to expand your platforms and portfolio.

Obviously, just a few and certainly not all at once, but over time, add several - one by one:

The first important one:

COURSES

Whatever you covered in your books, now turn it into a course and charge Premium prices for it.

Key here - as always - is getting the marketing part right. In this case, setting up an amazing launch and evergreen sequence that keeps money coming in while you sleep.

This is an elaborate process and not recommended for a total beginner, but once you've applied all the other techniques for a few months and have become more experienced with marketing and building an audience, you will be more than ready to add this awesome passive income stream to your portfolio.

It's important to understand:

Creating a course is the easy part!

Marketing it to evergreen success is where few succeed, and then often with phenomenal results (we are talking 6-7 figures) while most others fail.

The most successful way to market courses are webinars - live or pre-recorded (evergreen).

WEBINARS

Another powerhouse marketing tool, superbly effective for selling courses, softwares, coaching services, etc., but you have to learn how to do them well.

If you do, webinars can become a marketing tool like no other with amazing income streams for just an hour or 2 of work.

But it is a skill to be learned!

There is a specific presentation technique to well converting webinars and that is definitely not something you can figure out yourself.

Russell Brunson's "Perfect Webinar" template is amazing and he'll even send it to you for free - anywhere in the world.

You can order it here:

SassyZenGirl.com/Perfect-Webinar
(And yes, it's really free, incl. a DVD where he explains it to you)

PODCASTING or YOUTUBE

People LOVE podcasts and they LOVE video (even on social media now).

Pick one of the 2 and grow your brand.

These are some of the best trainings available *(see Resources Page)*.

My little Social Media book *(see Resources Page)*) also has an 10K-words Chapter on Youtube and what it takes to succeed there.

PODCAST GUESTING

Guesting on podcasts is another fantastic way to grow your brand awareness and tap into evermore audiences.

Landing guest spots is not that difficult, especially if you are an expert in your field. Podcasts are continuously looking for interesting guests to feature and will usually be quite interested in having you on.

To connect, check out iTunes podcasts and look through the bestsellers in your field. Check out their topics and listen to a few episodes to find the ones best suited and then contact them.

"News & Noteworthy" lists are another great area to scout for guest posting spots, especially in the beginning. Those are brand new podcasts who may not have a large following yet, but are eager to grow.

Keep in mind that guest podcasts - just like guest (blog) posts - are evergreen content. Meaning, people can find your episode for years to come which can bring a consistent stream of visitors to your website, blog, books, etc.

The same applies to new podcasts. While they might not have a lot of followers yet, some will grow and their incoming audiences will still have access to your interview.

To approach them, send an email, addressing them by name (don't do mass mails!) and write a few sentences about yourself, what you liked about their podcast (NOT generic, please!) and what subjects you could talk about (2-3 options).

Keep it short and give them some time to respond.

It's a number's game. The more people you approach, the more Yeses you will get.

Booking Guest spots is something you need keep doing on a continuous basis.

Be sure you have a lead magnet / freebie offer that you can share. The host will love that you give out free content to their audience and you get new subscribers to your mailing list!

eCOMMERCE & ETSY

If you are into arts and crafts, Etsy should be a main focus - and much sooner than step 7. Renea - one of the top sellers in this field - gives some awesome tips in her free video series.

An eCommerce store a la Shopify is another great monetization option, especially by focusing on products related to your passion. This again, you can start much sooner than Step #7, depending on your circumstances. It can also be an alternative (or addition) to affiliate marketing and niche sites.

Just like with any other field, finding that super specific sub niche that you can *dominate*, will be KEY to your success. Competition is HUGE and you will get lost in the masses, unless you position yourself for success. Here is Neil Patel's free in-depth beginner guide to setting up your first eCommerce store *(see Resources Page):*

Neil Patel: eCommerce - From Start to Profit

PINTEREST, TWITTER & INSTAGRAM

Now is definitely the time to fire up your social media!

Pick 2-3 maximum and become a marketing expert at each. For most businesses, I would recommend including at least one of the two: Pinterest or Instagram.

Their potential to reach and grow an audience is amazing and Pinterest pins are also very easy to rank in Google (and... - those pins don't grow old like on other social media platforms, instead permanently linking back to your site/blog... -> more traffic).
Here are two amazing resources to get you started:

FREE Instagram Training(*)

100K/month with Pinterest(*)

THE AWESOME POTENTIAL OF FACEBOOK GROUPS

You probably already have a Facebook page, but keep in mind that Facebook's algorithm is extremely restrictive: only 16% of your followers (if you are lucky) will actually get to see what you post!

Yep - you probably didn't know that, right?

It's a competition.

For a place in your follower's timelines.

All the other pages they follow will be competing with you and only very few are allowed through.

Why?

Because Facebook wants to make sure that users don't get overloaded with constant posts and the FB algorithm favors active, quality pages with VERY active engagement (comments, likes, shares) - and on a consistent basis.

No matter how hard you try, you will never reach all your followers and a much more efficient way to build relationships and an excited following are Facebook GROUPS (no competition there, every post will show in a member's timeline unless they change their notification settings).

Facebook Groups are absolutely amazing and much more personable than pages.

There is no other way to interact with your followers and clients that easily and naturally.

While your mailing list is your most important asset - because you own it - Facebook groups will be where the magic happens.

Where you can really actively help people and grow a passionate following - a "tribe".

I would put my energies more on a group (at least for Facebook) and then pick one or two more social platforms and really crush it there.

Give yourself at least a month or 2 to learn the most efficient techniques to grow a following on each. And then REALLY apply them consistently.

You will still need a Facebook page, also to run ads, and to keep that active, boost a few of your posts on a regular basis (see Chapter 5).

Once you figured out what works for you, you'll want to - once again - automate and outsource to some degree. Never completely, but enough to keep 90% of your time free for other things.

Social Media can be a big time sucker. That's why I placed them more at the end.

But now is the time to really hit them.

There are genre specific exceptions as I already mentioned: like travel, where Instagram is more important than anything.

Or arts & crafts where Pinterest is an absolute must.

To know which ones you should focus on, check out what the main influencers in your niche do and what *they* consider the most important marketing tool in their arsenal.

It will become obvious pretty quickly.

In the beginning, it's best to model after successful people, rather than reinventing the wheel.

Then, after you achieved a few successes and have more experience, by all means, start adding your own secret sauce.

But until then, take the direct route, the one others already paved for you - before becoming a trendsetter yourself.

SOFTWARE & MEMBERSHIPS

Long term you can also consider softwares, an app for your brand and a membership or subscription site.

You will know by then what will be most efficient and how to get started.

It's a nice carrot to look forward to…..

KEEP NETWORKING

That one never ends and the better you become at building relationships and creating win-win situations, the more successful you will be - and much faster.

Leveraging other people's audiences - both influencers and peers - can, once again, become a powerhouse marketing bonanza like few others.

Final Words

If you haven't already, be sure to claim the Bonus Course at a massive 50% Discount (limited time!) to create (or overhaul) an awesome looking and marketable website:

Design a Marketable Website or Blog
- in just a few hours -
even if you weren't born with a tech gene!

Go to: **SassyBlogBootcamp.com**

Also, join us in the friendliest Facebook group for newbie entrepreneurs. It's much easier when you share the journey with others and can get feedback and support.

Join HERE: **SassyZenGirl.Group**

What's your Passion?

Whatever you do, do it with flair and never lose sight of your passion!

Cherish that awesome enthusiasm and the amazing - once in a lifetime - adventure you are on!

It's a rare opportunity and congrats to you again for taking that first step!

You Rock!

In the beginning, there will be times where nothing seems to be working. When everyone seems to be successful while you can't even make 10 bucks online.

This is normal - and you are not special....;-) - at least not in that regard.

I was there many times during my first year.

Yes, I had it easier, because Kindle publishing jump started my online income, but I still had my share of frustrations as everyone does.

However, I HAD to make it work, because I was already traveling and there was NO WAY, I was going to give up my lifestyle or return to a "J-O-B".

Absolutely, NO WAY!

So I stuck with it - even when it was frustrating and when there seemed to be SO much to learn.

And then…

Suddenly….

It got easier.

And then a lot easier.

And while problems will always be a part of life and a part of business, you DO eventually reach a plateau where things get a lot more comfortable.

So hang in there and start with that mindset.

Give yourself at least a year without constantly stressing on success and turning this into money.

There is a good chance - a realistic chance - that it won't take that long.

Certainly a part-time income.

But you will get there a lot faster - and the journey will be much more enjoyable - if you don't pressure yourself so much and constantly expect results.

Think of planting a tree:

If you constantly dig up the roots and check for results, that poor tree will never have a chance.

Trust in the process.

If you do what is described here, you WILL get there.

Eventually.

And then it will be on stable ground.

Remember, this is still a LOT less time than any formal education would ever take.

And a MUCH larger earning potential (and passive income at that!).

Always keep that in mind.

You are going for the Holy Grail.

Financial freedom on your own terms.

And achieving it by doing something you love!

How awesome is that?

WHAT an amazing opportunity that we can even do this!

So:

Welcome aboard and I wish you much success and most of all **FREEDOM**.

You rock, my friend!

Over and out.

All the very best,
Gundi Gabrielle
SassyZenGirl.com
DreamClientsOnAutopilot.com

BONUS Chapter #1:
Marketing, Oh NO!!!
How to Chill with the M-Word

"Marketing isn't my thing...

I LOVE to create, but....not that sales stuff... It's just not my T-H-I-N-G..."

Ummm.

Whoopsie….

I've heard that *SO* many times!

Usually, from fabulously talented people with an absolute horror - almost dis-GUST - of marketing.

Yuk!

Sound like you?

Be honest… :)

I feel ya…

But let me ask you this:

You LOVE being broke?

This is a Biggie and something to keep in mind next time you bolt from the M-Word.

Ready?

Get this:

Once you see the first major BLING coming in from "M", you will start to **LOVE** her!

Absolutely ADORE her!

Become addicted to her!

Because here's the kicker:

Knowing how to crush it with "M" is what separates the millionaires in this "game" from the rest who barely make a buck *(because they are too "cool" to learn)!*

If you like being broke, stop reading right now!

Really.

You will be wasting your time.

IF, however, your are SICK of struggling and want your FREEDOM, I have good news for you, my friend:

There is a way out of the nightmare and it starts with the letter **M**.

Even better...

There are repeatable systems and methods you can ***LEARN!***

Whoa!

Yes, YOU, the one without the marketing gene (or so you think.....:).

It's simply learning how to do it, perfecting those methods and then - rinse and repeat.

Is there a learning curve?

You bet!

Will it be quick and easy?

Nope.

Will I have to work hard and apply myself?

Yep. You'll work your little booty off.

Will I be frustrated at times when nothing seems to work or I'm stuck with some super annoying tech problem (I'm SO non techie)?

Oh yea. You are getting the drift now…

B-U-T…

And this is one of the rare times, when the B-Word has any use at all.

When you DO and keep at it. Keep learning and keep improving until you become a MASTER-Ninja...

The sky in Cyberspace Wealthdom is literally *(not)* the limit!

That's not a sentimental cliche - nope - that's reality. And people prove it everyday.

Whatever you do. Whatever you want to share, no matter how awesome you are...

Unless you become a MASTER at marketing for whatever platform you use, **MUCHO BLING** will stay out of reach for **YOU**, my friend, for like EVER!

And wouldn't THAT suck?!

So:

Can we move past being silly and blushy around "M" - and finally allow her to help you **explode your brand**?

You have something awesome to share with the world, right?

Right…?

So share! - Let everyone know. Allow them to benefit from what you have to offer.

Because:

THAT's all Marketing really is!

Whewww…..really….?

M-hmm.

That's all it is.

Take a breath…

This was the most difficult part. You made it. Now let's rock:

Marketing is FUNNNNNN, Baby….!!

Yep, that's right.

When you understand how "M" really works and forget the sleazy salesman image - *which has **NADA** to* *do with marketing!* - then... "M" becomes **DELICIOUSLY AWESOME!**

Sassyliscious, really...

Gary Vaynerchuck, one of the most successful entrepreneurs and genius marketers of our time had this to say about "M":

"The Best Marketing Strategy in the World: CARE" - Gary Vaynerchuk

WOW!

Is *that* a different perspective - or what...?

How can you be sleazy and pushy - AND care for people at the same time?

That's right, you can't.

Marketing done right is about caring, building relationships and creating win-win situations for all sides.

It's about finding what people already *urgently* want - and then providing it to them => again, helping people.

But how? - You might ask.

And that's the other part that's holding y'all back:

The idea that marketing is difficult and complicated - and not something you could possibly EVER do.

Like it's some ultra secret Ninja science that only special people with the "marketing gene", enormous confidence and the gift of the gap can master.

Definitely NOT YOU!

EVER!

So you don't even try.

That ship has sailed. Why bother?

You are hopeless at marketing. That ugly word.....

RESET BUTTON

Big time!

Stop right now.

RE-SET!

Instead, let's look at the **5 pillars of FUN** - and effective - marketing and you will quickly see that YOU can absolutely master this.

That a lot of it is common sense and that it will actually be FUN - and even **FULFILLING**!

WHOA....

So let's hit it. Strap on your dancing boots and let's rock:

Oh.....one more side note:

Don't be so SERIOUS all the time!

Seriously. :)

Yes, you need to apply yourself and it will be quite a bit of work - BUT - nothing changes, just because you are having fun in the process.

Well…. actually it does - it will be MUCH easier for you and more fun for others to hear from you!

See how this works?

So, don't be a sourpuss or try to be super perfect. Perfect is boring.

Be YOU.

Full power, full steam you, like a force of nature and with laser focus.

But *never* without fun. Not ever!

Got it?

Cool - let's roll:

Pillar #1
Make it all about THEM

"What's in it for me?"

Wait? What? - I don't want to be selfish??

Relax. It's not about you.

This is the #1 concern any customer has when checking out your biz, service, book, blog - or whatever you offer.

We all do it and it's *not* selfish.

Time is precious. We may have a problem or frustration we need solved. And we want to find out quickly whether your product does.

That's the whole point after all.

So rather than reciting a long sales pitch that focuses on you, your product and all its awesome features, make it about THEM.

How will it improve/change THEIR lives. How will they FEEL after using your service or product?

Be crystal clear about the:

BEFORE and AFTER scenario

and paint a beautiful - *feeling* - picture of the AFTER - the result.

The more effectively you do, the more people will be pumped to check you out.

Well, not you…..your product…:)

Obviously, be genuine and don't make false promises. But if you truly believe in your product or service, this should be easy.

Again, don't recite why YOU believe in it. Make it about THEM and THEIR experience.

Pillar #2
Create Products/Services Customers urgently Want

Seems like a no brainer, but most never bother to find out what customers actually *want*.

Instead badgering them with endless sales pitches and telling them what they *should* want, which is rather patronizing, don't you think? - Let alone annoying.

How to find out?

Look at bestselling products or viral articles. **Buzzsumo** is a great free resource for the latter. And Amazon bestseller lists for products.

Most of all - **ASK** your existing readers/clients/customers. Frequently do a survey (people LOVE those), invite feedback in your autoresponder ("what is currently your biggest challenge?" or similar)

Read customer reviews of top selling products, especially the negative ones. They can often be a goldmine of ideas of what people find missing, what could be improved or added.

Again, make it all about THEM and....

Pillar #3
How can you best HELP them?

Rather than worrying about the sale or whether you can even make a sale, focus solely on how you can help that person. Maybe not even with your product.

Maybe it's not right for them. But rather than convincing them anyway - which is unethical - maybe you have a better suggestion that could really make a difference. Even if someone else makes that sale.

Don't you think that will build trust and loyalty? Don't you think they will come back to you next time they need something? And recommend you to everyone they know?

How rare is genuine selflessness these days?

Care, help and OVER-deliver and people will happily remember you and come back.

Caveat:
By "Help" I do NOT mean: solving their life's problems, serving as a free therapist or lending money. You need to value your time and not spend hours on this…. - in the few cases where it might be necessary, set clear boundaries and have an EXIT line prepared that's friendly and non-offensive, but gets you out the door. For everyone else: help and overdeliver.

Pillar #4
Don't view others as competitors

This is a super Biggie - and scary for many.

Get this:

NO ONE is like you!

Let that sink in....

I truly believe that everyone is AWESOME and has something special to offer that only *they* can share. It's just that most people never allow that part of them to shine and show - or don't even believe they have it.

Which is really sad.

EVERYBODY has something magical and unique about them.

So...

With that **SASSYLISCIOUS** insight, let's try again:

No one is like you, and if you create a product that you strongly believe in, that you created to help and support others, and.... that you can fully stand behind-.......you don't *ever* have to worry about competition.

Ever again!

WOW!

It get's better....

You ready?

Here it comes:

Rather than competing, see others as an endless sea of opportunities for collaboration. A win-win for both sides as well as for your audiences/customer base.

Keep breathing......

That way you can leverage each other's resources and following - and everyone will grow much faster.

WOW - what a concept!

There is room for everyone and if you are true to yourself, there will always be an audience and a following for you. Specifically you.

Constantly network and build relationships - unselfishly. The more you do, the faster you will grow.

And while there will be the occasional BooBoo who doesn't "get it", many others will and y'all can grow together.

Don't be mad at the BooBoo's. They just don't know better. And it's tough being a BooBoo and being arrogant and competitive all the time. Exhausting really....

I'm flat just thinking about it....

So feel for them - just for a sec - and then move on with a smile.

Because YOU, my friend, are ON your way!

Pillar #5
Share the True You

Yep - there had to be some fluff in this post....;)

Bear with me... here it goes:

BE genuine.

And be true to yourself.

Don't try to blend in or be like everyone else.

The world needs you.

Yes, YOU!

The unique, true you - not the cookie cutter persona most of us present to the world to be liked and fit in.

Fitting in is overrated. And it's boring!

Be generous with us. Share how awesome you really are.

And no "BUTs".

Strike that word from your vocabulary.

Like FOREVER!

And then let that boundless enthusiasm burst through that you've been holding back all those years.

Who gives a booty whether you do it "right"?

Have a blast with it. Enjoy your awesome uniqueness, and that way we all can, too.

You have something to share with the world.

Yes, YOU. The shy one in the back.

Time to come out of your shell and LET IT RIP!

Make this the most awesome ride of your life - and FLY!

BONUS Chapter #2:
Sassyliscious Brand Explosion - Say wha...?

What the booty is a "Brand"? - and why do I need one?

Superliscious question!

Why indeed?

Well....

Actually, you don't - *"need"* - a brand.

You **ARE** - the brand.

Whoa!

Ummm.

Wha'..?

I don't get it…?

Yep.

Your brand is an expression of **WHO** you are and what drives you…

aka **WHY** - you do what you do.

mhhh…..

wha…?

I know….

Super fluff….;-)

But bear with me - there is a point here...

First, let's trash one mega boo-boo myth:

Do you need to spend thousands of dollars and hire an expensive PR firm to create your brand?

Yo, NO. Not cool!

Not at all!

You - and only you - can create YOUR brand successfully, and it's one of THE most FUN parts of entrepreneurship and building a business.

Ready?

Let's do this:

So WHO are you?

No, seriously.

More importantly:

WHY are you **passionate** about your biz/ product / niche?

You are passionate, right...?

Otherwise, what's the point?

So tell me - *I mean that* - tell me:

Why are you so *passionate* about your business/ product?

What do you *LOVE to share* with your customers/audience?

What are you hoping *their experience* will be like when they read your book or blog, use your product for the first time or have their first session with you?

Whatever it may be.

NOPE - don't think!

Just *FEEL* into it and then tell me. Excitedly! - Like when you first conceived your awesome project.

Don't try to be perfect. Perfect is boring.

You can share in the comments below - I will definitely read it.

In the meantime, record while you tell me or invite a good friend over for coffee and tell them.

Or tell your doggy or kitty. They are great for this…:)

Share how *PRECIOUS* this is to you and why.

Again, either record it or have the friend give you feedback.

You can also send me an imaginary email...;) - I'm only half kidding...

Ummm, seems odd, why are we doing this? I feel silly...

Well....because once you do and get over yourself. Once you start speaking from your heart and let your enthusiasm ***EXPLODE***, you will notice certain words and patterns coming up.

Choices of words that are very unique and specific. And usually very beautiful.

When you speak with enthusiasm, you speak from your heart and the true you comes through - not the cookie cutter fit-in version that most people present to the world.

THAT's who we want to see.

And that's where your brand will come from. It's actually already in there, you just have to unveil it.

Yep.

That simple.

So enjoy that little process and do it a few times if you are self-conscious at first.

Then write down the words that stood out. In particular power words that carry strong emotions.

Here is a whole epic list of power words to give you an idea of what I mean *(see Resources Page)*.

Generic is Boo-Boo

I can't say it often enough, but generic is BOOring and businesses with generic marketing usually don't last long.

We are SO tired of seeing the *same old/same old* over and *OVER* again - and absolutely LOVE when someone brings a breath of fresh air to their branding and personality.

Even goes against the "rules" and creates something completely new.

This makes branding really easy.

And **FUN**!

You just have to be you.

Ummm....

Whoa.....

I dunno.....

You might say.

I'm really not that interesting and isn't that just totally selfish and self-centered?

Nope.

It's not.

You are doing everyone a favor by bringing out the true, awesome, real you, instead of the cookie cutter carbon copy you have been showing to the world.

Most people never realize how awesome and interesting they are.

How much they have to share.

And that's a pity.

Because the world is all the poorer for it.

So, be generous.

Do us all a favor and share the awesome you. The REAL you and all that you are passionate about.

You have something amazing to give. Deep down you know that.

So please GIVE.

If you need help digging deeper, try these 2 resources:

23 Powerful Questions to Awaken your Passion and Find your True Purpose:
SassyZenGirl.com/Find-Your-Passion-Purpose

Evan Carmichael: Your One Word

Supercool Example:

One of my readers was struggling to find a tagline for her new Etsy business.

She had started to come up with some examples and was dreading the process. She initially came up with a rather generic line about how her soaps were helping people, nothing exciting really.

Even though she was *working* hard on it.

And that was just it!

She was *working* on it. Laboring over it, when it should really be fun.

Then I discovered an email she had sent me a while back. At the time, she was about to start her first blog and had asked my advice on whether she should focus on nursing, since that's what she was teaching professionally - or follow her passion.

You can probably guess my answer and then I got this reply from her:

"I REALLY want to bring more fun and color and creativity to people"

WOW!

How is that for passion and inspiration?

What a beautiful choice of words and it came from her heart and soul.

Fun - Color - Creativity

What an unusually fun way to describe soaps and bath products.

I love it.

I want to buy right now!

Her soap creations were an expression of her passion to bring "more fun, color and creativity" to people's lives!

See how different and amazing that is than a generic description?

Who would not line up to buy those soaps?

Now we suddenly have an *feeling* image with them - a beautiful scene. Something we will always remember when we look at them. And it was genuinely and uniquely her.

3 beautiful words that stimulate joy and happiness...

When I mentioned this to her, she replied:

"I realized "color, fun & creativity" would also carry over to teaching and writing to inspire others. ***Tapping into the creative side of my brain has helped me find balance and I hope to empower or inspire others to find that for themselves as well.*** *Soaps may seem so simple, but they are so much fun to make and design. And I love when they make someone feel special."*

And - wow - another amazing line and expression of her true essence:

"I love when they make someone feel special."

See how these seemingly little statements changed her entire brand and how people perceive her products.
Now when I think of her products - the same products as before - I think how special they will make me feel, because they were handcrafted with such *love*. They bring color, fun and creativity to my life. And what could be more awesome than that?

Most of all, it wasn't a catchy marketing line - although it could be - it was genuine. And that's what touches people. All of us, even when we don't know why.

Another interesting word she mentioned was *"**Balance**"* and how being creative brought balance to her life.

You think that could be woven into the product description and whole brand/marketing strategy?

You betcha....

These soaps bring **calmness** to my life. **Relaxation. Balance.**

WOW - I'm so ready to buy them now. Really (and you can, too, **over here**...;-) *(see Resources page)*.

She suddenly enjoyed the process, too, and said - "this is so much fun."

Not tedious, awful marketing. Your boring homework that you have to get done.

No - it was a wonderful exploration.

She realized things about herself that she didn't even know and the results were mesmerizing.

How much FUN will you have with this?

BONUS Sassy Pointer

Include YOUR favorite Colors

I once had my aura photo taken.

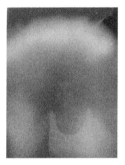

Yep - I admit - and before you laugh, the machine was actually developed by Nicola Tesla!

There is, of course, plenty of scientific proof that there is such a thing as an aura, an energy field around us that is a coloric reflection of our essence. who we are. It usually comes with a specific color pattern and it can change throughout life.

I was shocked when I saw mine, because it was the perfect expression and combination of my favorite color palette. The one I feel absolutely in sync with and *nurtured* by.

Holy Wow!

No worries, you don't need to get your aura picture taken...:) - but you know, of course, what your favorite colors are. The ones you deeply resonate with. That nurture you and make you feel awesome every time you see them.

I can't walk past anything that's pink. I'm completely addicted to that color and it's a beautiful, nurturing feeling.

Obviously, I made it a major part of the *SassyZenGirl* brand and it's been awesome.

It gives me a rush every time I see it!

Does everybody like it?

Nope.

Does it matter?

Nope.

Why would it?

You'll never please everyone and you don't need to, but you *will* attract the people who resonate on a similar frequency as you - and they don't all have to love pink…:)

THAT's why the thought of competition is silly.

If you are really, truly you - and your brand *truly* reflects that - there will be *no one like you* and you will never have to worry about competition again.

Be a generic cookie-cutter BooBoo and the C word will always be a big problem for you, because generic is boring. You'll always need to fight for survival and you'll never quite get there.

So enjoy this **EXPLORATION**.

Have **FUN** with the **ADVENTURE** and have you and your brand melt into one awesome, unique expression of YOU!

Whoa - SUPER fluff - but cool…:)

More SassyZenGirl Yummies

COURSES

SassyZenGirl's Blogging Bootcamp
SassyBlogBootcamp.com

FREE Masterclass:
POWER MARKETING BLUEPRINT
DreamClientsOnAutopilot.com

Award Winning
INFLUENCER FAST TRACK
Series

#1 Bestselling
BEGINNER INTERNET MARKETING
Series
"The Sassy Way... when you have NO CLUE!"

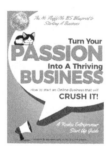

#1 Bestselling
TRAVEL BOOKS

Score FREE Flights, Rental Cars & Accommodations. Dramatically reduce Airfares. Get paid to Travel & START a DIGITAL NOMAD BIZ you can run from anywhere in the world!

ZEN TRAVELLER
BALI
A QUICK GUIDE

Explore the "real" Bali…
The quiet, magical parts
far away from the
tourist crowds…

About the Author

Gundi Gabrielle, aka *SassyZenGirl*, loves to explain complex matters in an easy to understand, fun way. Her *"The Sassy Way...when you have NO CLUE!!"* series has helped thousands around the world conquer the jungles of internet marketing with humor, simplicity and some sass.

A 11-time #1 Bestselling Author, Entrepreneur and former Carnegie Hall conductor, Gundi employs marketing chops from all walks of life and loves to help her readers achieve their dreams in a practical, fun way. Her students have published multiple #1 Bestsellers outranking the likes of Tim Ferris, John Grisham, Hal Elrod and Liz Gilbert.

When she is not writing books or enjoying a cat on her lap (or both), she is passionate about exploring the world as a Digital Nomad, one awesome adventure at a time.

She has no plans of settling down anytime soon.

SassyZenGirl.com
SassyZenGirl.Group
DreamClientsOnAutopilot.com

Instagram.com/SassyZenGirl
Youtube.com/c/SassyZenGirl
Facebook.com/SassyZenGirl
Twitter.com/SassyZenGirl

Made in the USA
Columbia, SC
03 February 2022

55300085R00085